A Kid's Guide to Boise

Rick Just

Copyright © 2018 by Rediscovered Publishing
All rights reserved. This book or any portion thereof may not be reproduced or used in any manner whatsoever without the express written permission of the publisher except for the use of brief quotations in a book review.

Printed in the United States of America

Cover and interior design: Kelly Knopp
Interior layout: Jane Alice Van Doren
Editor: Laura Wally Johnston

First Printing, 2018

ISBN: 978-0-9988909-4-4

Rediscovered Publishing
180 N 8th Street
Boise, Idaho 83712

www.rediscoveredpublishing.com

OFFICE OF THE MAYOR

David H. Bieter

January 10, 2018

Dear Friends,

Boise is a great place for families, so of course, it's terrific for kids. We have places to play that few other cities can match, and Boise has developed a national reputation as a premier destination for recreation of all kinds.

Grab your skateboard and head to Rhodes Skate Park where the X-Games competitors ride, or switch to a stand-up paddleboard at Quinn's Pond. Head up to Bogus Basin for winter skiing and scream down the mountain on the brand new "Glade Runner" mountain coaster. Take a walk or ride your bike down the 25-mile Boise Greenbelt that runs alongside the Boise River, one of the most beautiful urban streams in the nation. Visit the MK Nature Center to see the beauty of the river up close, or view the world from the sky through the eyes of a raptor at the World Center for Birds of Prey.

Go to prison! Yes, really. Visiting the Old Idaho Penitentiary is an unforgettable experience. From hiking and mountain biking in our picture postcard Foothills, to rafting or fishing in the Boise River and Lucky Peak, there is always something to do in Boise! The Idaho State Museum, the Basque Block, the Capitol Building, the Discovery Center, the Boise Depot, almost 100 different parks... I could go on and on about all the wonderful things Boise has to offer, however I don't need to. The Kid's Guide to Boise will tell you all about this city that I love. Have fun!

Sincerely,

David H. Bieter
Mayor

BOISE CITY HALL: 150 North Capitol Boulevard | MAIL: P.O. Box 500, Boise, Idaho, 83701-0500
P: 208-972-8520 | F: 208-384-4420 | TDD/TTY: 800-377-3529

CITYOFBOISE.ORG

Table of Contents

Map 1
Map Key & How to use this book . . 2
Public Art 4
Statehouse 8
Basques 12
Jump 14
Events 16
Celebrations 20
Fun Food 22
Show Me 28
Anne Frank 33
Museums 34
City of Trees 37
Inside Out 39
Zoo Boise 42

Ridge to Rivers	44
Wheels	48
Winging It	50
Fins	54
Splash	56
Up There	60
Hot	62
Weapons	66
Creepy	68
Parks	70
Bogus	72
Winter	74
Book It	76
Climbing	78
Pro Sports	80
Family Fun	82
North End	84
Bowns Crossing	87

In the Desert 88
Camping 90
Cemetaries 92
Ghost Towns 94
On the Edge 96
Icons 98
Souvenirs 102
Walking Around 104
Time Out 106
Bucket List 108
Index 110

Map Key

1. Bogus Basin
2. Camel's Back
3. North End
4. Rhode's Skate Park
5. JUMP
6. Anne Frank Memorial
7. Library!
8. Downtown Boise
9. Fountain at the Grove
10. Boise River
11. Boise Greenbelt
12. Boise Depot
13. Capitol Blvd. Bridge
14. State Capitol
15. Foothills Learning Center
16. Idaho State Museum
17. Boise Art Museum
18. Morrison Center
19. BSU Campus
20. Bronco Stadium
21. Zoo Boise
22. MK Nature Center
23. Botanical Garden
24. Old Penetentiary
25. Table Rock
26. Lucky Peak
27. Discovery Center

Boise by the numbers:

Population: About 229,000 in the city limits	Average summer high: 90.2
Elevation: 2,840 feet above sea level	Average winter low: 21.6
Area: 64 square miles	Annual precipitation: 12.1 inches
Average sunny days: 234	Average snowfall: 21.3 inches

How to Use This Book

Check the table of contents to find a subject you're interested in or discover new things to love by reading the guide start to finish. You can always head to the index at the back if you're looking for something specific.

Don't forget to make use of our adventure planning sections:
- Walking Around (pg. 104) will tell you things to experience that are close together
- Time Out! (pg. 106) can help you make a plan based on the time you have to spend
- Boise Bucket List (pg. 108) has recommendations and space for you to make your own must-see list.

Have fun out there!

Public Art

Spring Run

Don't touch it! You hear that, sometimes, right? Well, you can touch the public art in Boise. This art installation is called Spring Run. It has six cast-metal bear heads sticking out of the side of the building at 121 9th Street making an upside-down pyramid. Supposedly you can rub the nose of the bear on the bottom for good luck. While you're back there, look up to see the ceramic fish swimming above the bears.

Utility Boxes

Every corner that has a traffic light also has a big, metal box that contains all the wiring and controls for that light. They're usually ugly, except in Boise. More than 160 of the Boise boxes have art on them. Artists don't paint on the boxes. They come up with a design, get it approved by Boise City Arts and History, then send it to a company that creates a "wrap." You see advertising wraps on cars, trucks, and buses. Now you see art wraps on those much-better-looking metal boxes.

Centennial

Idaho turned 100 years old in 1990. To help celebrate that centennial, Idaho's 44 counties were asked to send in their county emblem to be put on light poles in Boise. Some counties didn't have an emblem, so they had to get one designed in a hurry. You'll see them if you look up at the street lights on Capitol Boulevard. Most of them show what each county is famous for.

HONEST ABE

Everybody wants a photo with Lincoln. In Boise, you have a couple of choices. You can stand by the Lincoln statue in front of the capitol building and take a selfie. He's way up there on a pedestal, so that won't be so hot. The all-time best chance for a picture with Abraham is in Julia Davis Park. There's a GIANT Lincoln sitting on a bench there waiting for a picture with you. The original sculpture was done by (funny name alert) Gutzon Borglum, the same guy who did the faces on Mount Rushmore. Borglum was born in Idaho.

Freak Alley

Freak Alley Gallery got started when a business owner caught a guy drawing a picture on his back door with a felt tip pen. Did the owner get mad? Nope. He liked the picture, so he let the guy keep on drawing. Other artists asked if they could paint murals in the alley. Building owners said, "It's just an alley, go ahead." Now the whole ally is covered with art. The artists decide who gets to paint there. They do new murals every August, painting at night using flood lights so they can see what they're doing. Most artists use spray paint, even for fine detail. They can make a skinny little line by spraying through a pinhole punched in a piece of cardboard.

Statehouse

Old 97

A minor piece of Civil War history rests quietly on the grounds of the Idaho Statehouse. It's a 42-pound seacoast gun, a cannon used during the Civil War at Vicksburg. The gun was forged in 1857. At the top of the muzzle rim "No. 97" is stamped. It has been known as "Old Ninety-Seven" and as "Model 1840". The "42-pound" refers to the weight of the cannonball, not the weight of the cast iron gun. It has never been fired in Idaho. Officially. Pranksters set off some powder in it a couple of times before the state sealed it up.

Boise is the capital of Idaho. That's capital, spelled with two A's. The building that you see at the end of Capitol Boulevard (spelled with an O replacing that second A) is Idaho's capitol building. When referring to the building, you spell capitol with an O. An easy way to remember is that many capitol buildings have a round space under the dome called a rotunda. That round space is shaped like an O, right? Idaho's capitol building has been in use since 1905, though it has been updated a couple of times.

The Elevator

When the center part of the capitol was built in 1905, the part with the dome, you could ride a special elevator to the fourth floor where the Idaho Supreme Court met. Over the years the wings were added to the building for the Idaho House and Senate. Sometime during a remodel of the building the elevator was covered up. They found it again during renovation in 2007. It doesn't work today, but it is so pretty they decided to open it up so you can see it. It's easy to miss, so be sure you ask where the old elevator is.

The Vault

No, we don't keep state employees locked up during working hours in Idaho. There are a couple of vault doors in the statehouse that lead to offices. These doors used to lead to vaults full of money and gold, but Idaho keeps its money in banks now. Banks work just fine as a place to keep Idaho's money today, so they aren't needed. The vault doors were kept in place when the capitol was remodeled just because they look so cool.

Winged Victory

The statue on the fourth floor is a plaster replica of the marble statue Nike of Samothrace, often called Winged Victory. The original is in the Louvre in Paris. It is part of a collection the city of Paris sent to the United States after World War II to thank our country for our help in that war. Each state got a Merci Car filled with artwork and mementos. Merci means thank you in French.

A Great Seal

Idaho has the only state seal designed by a woman. Emma Edwards Green won a contest to design the seal for the new state in 1891. The prize was $100. The seal, which was changed a bit in 1957, also appears on the state flag. The mosaic seal on the floor of the garden level of the statehouse is the only part of the floor that isn't marble. The more than 9,000 pieces of glass for the mosaic were cut on site.

Washington

Charles Ostner had some patience. It took him four years to carve the wooden statue of George Washington astride a horse that stands on the fourth floor of the statehouse. Ostner modeled the statue in snow before committing it to pine. He studied the likeness of George Washington on a postage stamp to get the face right. Ostner donated the statue to the State of Idaho in 1869. It stood outside the statehouse for 65 years, before it was brought inside and gilded (covered with gold leaf or gold paint).

State Capitol by the numbers:

There are:
340 steps in the rotunda
219 pillars
350 windows in the building

Height of the building from the ground to the top of the eagle:
208 ft tall.

The eagle itself is covered in gold leaf and stands 5' 7".

Boise has one of the largest populations of people with a Basque heritage in the United States. Even our mayor is Basque!

Boise's Basques

The Basque Block

There are around 16,000 Basques in Boise. They live all over town, not in a particular area. They do have one special place where they can get together to celebrate their culture, and you're invited. It's called the Basque Block - it's on West Grove Street between Capitol Boulevard and South 6th Street. You can't miss it because the street is painted red and green with interesting designs reflecting Basque culture. There's a Basque market, Basque restaurants, the Basque Museum, the Basque Center, and a pelota court. Pelota is a type of handball often played by Basques.

The Basques lived in Europe for centuries in the Basque Country on both sides of the border between northwestern Spain and southwestern France. They often made their living on the sea. Many members of Columbus' crew were Basque sailors.

Some of the first Basques to immigrate to Idaho became sheepherders.

Jaialdi

Jaialdi means "Festival" in Euskara (the Basque Language). This festival exhibits the Basque culture with dancing (dantzan) and musical (musika) performances, sporting (kirol) events, and authentic food (jateko) and drink (edateko). Jaialdi was first celebrated in 1987 as a one-time weekend event to educate the public about the Basque culture. The festival was so popular that Governor Cecil Andrus asked the local Basque community to put on another celebration for Idaho's Centennial in 1990. That went so well that Jaialdi is now celebrated every five years. The next one is scheduled for July 28 - August 2, in 2020.

Basque Museum and Boarding House

The Basque Museum and Cultural Center exhibits change regularly to tell the surprising story of Basques in Idaho. You might see a sheepherder's wagon, learn about the traditional dress of the dancers, or voyage with the crew of Columbus.

Next door is the oldest brick house still standing in Boise, and the first to have a bathtub. It became a Basque boarding house in the early 1900s. You can see the bowling area (it's outside), and a pelota court. Ask about the archeological dig beneath the side porch.

Jacobs Family, ca. 1880

JUMP

It's safe to say there is nothing else like JUMP, anywhere. J.R. Simplot made his first millions in agriculture. His company perfected the process that gives you the French fries you order at a fast food restaurant. He was fascinated by old tractors, and he wanted to share his collection of those with the public. After Mr. Simplot passed away, the J.R. Simplot Foundation wanted to display his vintage tractors. But they wanted to do more than that.

JUMP is a metaphor for "explorative" play. It's also an acronym. JUMP stands for Jack's Urban Meeting Place. The play part means you can slide down the five-story spiral slide, or race your friends side-by-side on the 8-person team slide, or crawl around like a spider in The Climber, which also looks like a piece of art.

The explore part of JUMP is where you can take classes, and use the maker space equipment such as the video studio and 3D printers. The art is worth a trip in itself, and they host dozens of special events. Did we mention the tractors? Machinery, man! Take a tour of the 50 tractors, many powered by steam like a locomotive.

Events

Spirit of Boise Balloon Classic

You can often see hot air balloons over Boise during the summer. On Labor Day Weekend, you can't miss them. That's when the Spirit of Boise Balloon Classic takes place. You'll see dozens of balloons, including some that are shaped like cartoon characters. Balloons are just a big bag of hot air. That bag is called the envelope. Dangling beneath is the gondola that holds the people. The pilot heats the air inside the envelope by increasing or decreasing a flame (much like a welding torch).

Twilight Criterium

A special kid event takes place in mid July every year when Olympic Gold Medalist Kristin Armstrong leads the kids' ride that opens the Twilight Criterium cycling event. Some of the best bicyclists in the world race in front of thousands of spectators.

Western Idaho Fair

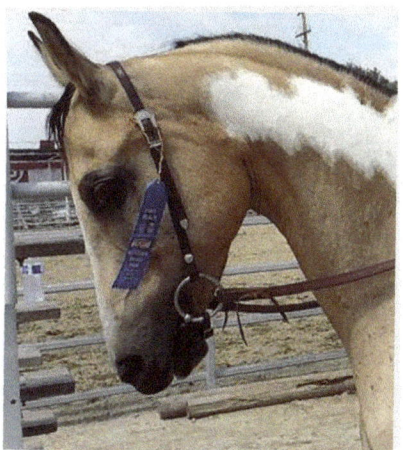

Have you ever been to a real country fair? The Western Idaho Fair has all the midway rides and games you could want, yummy food, and animals to see. It takes place every August in Garden City, just a few minutes from downtown. Plan to spend the day there. Maybe the evening, too. There are always great concerts booked.

Engineering and Science Festival

The Engineering and Science Festival held every February at Boise State University has dozens of free activities for K-12 kids. Meet scientists and engineers and ask them about their jobs. Participate in hands on activities.

Treefort

The organizers of Treefort remembered how cool it was when they were kids to have a place they could hang out. They nailed the name Treefort to their music fest like a "Kids Only" sign on a treehouse! It is such a cool place to hang out. They have dozens of bands playing for five days in March at various venues all over town. It's not just about music, though. They have Foodfort, Comedyfort, Hackfort, Filmfort, Skatefort, Storyfort, and Yogafort. Many of the events are family friendly, plus check out Kidfort.

Comic Arts Festival

If you're into superheroes, villains, and comics, you can't miss the Comic Arts Festival! You'll meet illustrators, authors, and you'll have a chance to do a little cosplay. It's different every year, so check the Library! website for dates and events.

Frisbee Fest

Dogs have been flying through the air after Frisbees every September for more than 25 years at the annual Frisbee Fest in Ann Morrison Park, sponsored by Zamzows to benefit the Idaho Humane Society. Their trained humans throw the Frisbee and the dogs catch them, sometimes 200 feet out! That's for the distance contest. There are also prizes for style. It costs a little to enter your dog, but anyone can watch the competition for free. Pro tip: Bring folding chairs.

See Spot Walk

Every October thousands of dogs and their people participate in a fundraiser for the Idaho Humane Society called See Spot Walk. You'd think with all those dogs there would be a lot of barking and growling. Not much. There are so many dogs (all on leashes) that each dog feels a little overwhelmed. There is a lot of tail wagging and sniffing though. In addition to the walk, there are vendors there with all kinds of dog stuff for sale. You'll probably see a doggie fashion show and some dogs showing off what they know, often on an agility course.

Art in the Park

The weekend following Labor Day Weekend every year more than 200 artists gather in Julia Davis Park for Art in the Park. It's free and it's fun. You'll see art of every kind, and get to participate in art activities for kids. You won't starve, either. Food vendors are scattered throughout the booths. Pro tip: Leave your dog at home.

CELEBRATIONS

Parades

If parades are your thing, you're in luck if it's November. Boise puts on both a Holiday Parade, and a Veterans Day Parade downtown in November.

Halloween at Linder Farms

You won't find a farm in downtown Boise. You can find one 23 minutes from town that is a special attraction around Halloween. They have a 20-acre pumpkin patch, and a corn maze that turns into the Trail of Terror around Halloween. They have hay rides, a straw bale maze, a tractor tire playground, a petting zoo, pedal tractors, a bounce house, a barrel train ride, and a giant slide. Meanwhile, if you're all about trick or treating, check out the big houses along Harrison Boulevard. They really put on a show for Halloween.

Scentsy Commons Christmas Lights

Scentsy is a company that makes things that smell terrific. The headquarters for Scentsy is in Meridian, about 13 minutes from downtown Boise. They turn their campus into a gigantic light show during the holidays. How gigantic? Forty-three miles of lights. That's more than 700,000 of them.

Festival of Trees

St. Alphonsus Hospital has been putting on a Festival of Trees for more than 30 years. Families, nonprofits, schools, and businesses compete to come up with the best-decorated trees for the festival. There is continuous entertainment from dance groups, choirs, and musicians each day, along with special events such as a fashion show.

Idaho Potato Drop

Sure, they have that big crystal ball that they drop in Times Square in New York City, but nobody celebrates the New Year like we do in Boise. At the stroke of midnight, the spotlights are on the enormous Idaho potato that descends dramatically from the arm of a giant crane. People yell and scream and have fun. Bands play. Fireworks go off. It's a Happy New Year!

Winter Garden Aglow

Why would you go to a garden in the winter? Mostly because of the 390,000 holiday lights they have strung around the trees and through the bushes and across the arches at Winter Garden Aglow at the Idaho Botanical Garden. You're also likely to see Santa, and a G-scale model train called the Holiday Express winding through it all. Bonus: Hot chocolate!

Fun Food

The STIL

So, can you hear me screaming? You know, for ice cream? The STIL in downtown Boise's BODO has totally screamable ice cream. STIL stands for Sweetest Things In Life. They're very convincing about that. They make all their ice cream on site using fresh ingredients, mostly from Idaho. Some of their ice cream names are Carribbean Cruise, Grandpa's Laugh, Licking the Spoon, After School Special, White Elephant, and Idaho Wilderness. But, you can probably just ask for chocolate. Ooh, or maybe chocolate peppermint, or peanut butter cookies, or...

Idaho Spud Bars

Idaho is famous for potatoes, so it may not surprise you that we have a potato candy bar. It isn't made from spuds, it just looks like one. The Idaho Spud bar is made by the Idaho Candy Company. They have a cocoa flavored, soft marshmallow center and are covered with dark chocolate and sprinkled with coconut. They have been making them since 1918, and you can find them in the candy section of almost every grocery store in Boise.

Guru Donuts

Your average, plain ol' everyday donut is pretty good, right? There's nothing average about the treats at Guru Donuts downtown. They have donuts with almond toffee covered in chocolate fudge, bacon covered maple glaze donuts, a donut called Santa's Milk & Cookies, donuts with eggnog pastry cream, and dozens more. If you're into donuts and stories, every Tuesday they have Tasty Tales Story Time. It's a 20-minute story session at 10 am, and they do it again at 10:30. Participants get a special donut deal with milk or chocolate milk.

The Kabob House

A kabob is a skewer of roasted meat, fish or vegetables. It's a popular way of preparing foods in the Middle East. The owner of the Kabob House in Boise is from Afghanistan. He can spear up some tasty kabobs for you, while you enjoy the colorful fabrics and pillows in the plush booth.

Leku Ona

The Basque culture is important to Boise (see page 12). Do you want to try Basque food? Leku Ona on the Basque Block serves lunch and dinner. You can sample street tacos, fried calamari, lamb stew, beef tongue, salmon, tripe and more. The owner grew up in the Basque Country and knows their cuisine well.

DOG BISCUITS

Now this is fun food. It's not for you, though. B'ARC Peanut Butter Bones are for your favorite dog. They are made right here in Boise from all natural ingredients that even people could eat. Don't. They're for your DOG, who will love them. They're made without preservatives by people with disabilities at an organization called The Arc. You can get them at the Idaho Humane Society and some area pet stores.

TANGO'S

Do you know what an empanada is? Do you know how to pronounce em-pah-nah-da? They're a closed bread dish something like a sandwich. Many cultures have them. They're called calzones in Italy, piroshkis in Russia, pasties in England, and empanadas in Argentina. Want to try the Argentina version? Tango's can make that happen with two locations in Boise and one in Nampa. They stuff them with what you like and make them while you wait. Don't forget to order a dessert empanada!

Flying Pie

Have you seen pies fly? At Flying Pie Pizza they are famous for throwing pizza dough spinning into the air and usually catching it. They serve "Whirled Famous Pizzas." They do special pizza tours where you can learn how pizzas are made while making one for yourself. It takes about an hour, so you'll be so ready to eat when yours comes out of the oven. They'll even teach you how to fold up the box so you can take it home.

Kibrom's Restaurant

New words! New food! Injera is like a large, spongy pancake. It's the centerpiece of Ethiopian food, and it's like a plate you can eat. They pile spicy vegetables and meaty stews onto the injera, then you tear off little pieces and scoop up the good stuff like you're building a mini-taco. The owners are from Eritrea, which is a small country on the horn of Africa.

Boise Fry Company

They flip things here. Yeah, burgers get flipped, but so does the menu. Fries are the big deal and you order a burger on the side, if you like. They make fries from different kinds of spuds, Russet, gold, laura, yams, sweet, purple, Okinawa, and whatever is in season. Once you've picked your potato, you get to tell them how you want your fries, regular, homestyle, curly, shoestring, or Po' Balls. They'll explain that last one.

Show Me

Egyptian Theater

Walk into the Egyptian Theater and within about a second your head will tip back and your jaw will drop open. In 1922 archaeologists had uncovered the tomb of Egyptian King Tutankhamun, or King Tut. All things Egyptian became the rage, so in 1927 developers built the Egyptian Theater in Boise. You'll see reproductions of hieroglyphs on the pillars and over the stage, with golden statues on either side. Look for the grillwork above the statues. If you peek inside you can see the pipes of a massive pipe organ that they still play on special occasions. You can see movies at the Egyptian, attend concerts, or listen to readings by authors. Whatever reason you're there, half the fun is just looking up. If the doors are open, ask if you can look around.

Boise Contemporary Theater

Are you an actor, or would you like to be one? Check out Boise Contemporary Theater's (BCT) Theater Lab. Small teams of students age 12-18 work together with professional actors to create a play. They write it, work it, rewrite it, then produce it. Ten-week sessions run each Spring and Fall.

Do you just like to hear stories? BCT has a children's reading series for those six and above where professional actors bring the best contemporary children's theater to life. Bonus: free milk and cookies or free pizza.

See the Idaho Shakespeare Festival

If you want to see great theater, the Idaho Shakespeare Festival has a deal for kids. The first Sunday of each production during the season is Family Night, the only night kids under 6 are admitted and a special youth price is offered for kids under 12.

Shakespeare could come to you. The Festival brings fully produced live theater to schools through Idaho and neighboring states with its Idaho Theater for Youth and Shakespearience School tours.

Be the Idaho Shakespeare Festival

Do you want to get up on that stage? The School of Theater has classes for everyone, Pre-K to adult. It's different every session, but classes such as Story Theater, Page to Stage, Broadway Basics, Clowning Around, Improv, and Performance Intensives are available. Summer camps are offered throughout the entire summer. Want to be a part of the company? Look into the high school Apprentice Program!

Boise Philharmonic Youth Orchestra

Do you have musical talent? The Boise Philharmonic Youth Orchestra is the Treasure Valley's premier performing youth symphonic group. The group is open to woodwind, brass, percussion, and string 9th-12th grade students by audition. Student musicians receive coaching from principal players of the Boise Philharmonic. The Youth Orchestra performs three concerts per year, with programs selected to broaden young musicians' fluency with the enduring masterworks.

Story Story Night

Electric. Illuminating. Inspiring. Story Story Night is a live storytelling program that lets the community share real experiences, live on stage and without notes. With a wide range of shows, studios and storytellers, Story Story Night fosters powerful connections that change lives through the courageous act of true storytelling. The all-ages flagship season runs November through April at JUMP in downtown Boise. (Parental discretion advised.)

Opera Idaho

Opera Idaho has been performing in the Treasure Valley for over 40 years, and now performs across the state. If you enjoy opera, you can catch their performances at the Egyptian Theater. If you want to perform, they have two children's choruses, one for grades 2 through 5, and one for grades 6 through 10.

Ballet Idaho

Ballet Idaho Academy (BIA) is the official school of Ballet Idaho and is the only ballet school in the Intermountain West to have a professional ballet company affiliation. BIA offers classes from ages 3+ in pointe, contemporary, jazz, tap, hip-hop, and ballet, including an extensive beginning and intermediate adult program.

Boise Music Week

Boise has been celebrating Music Week in May since 1919, with Broadway musicals, chorale groups, rock bands, orchestras, and more. Most performances take place at the Velma V. Morrison Center for the Performing Arts. Everything is free. You can be in the audience, or try out for a performance.

Boise Little Theater

Boise Little Theater is Idaho's longest running, all volunteer, community theater. They produce several plays a year that are fun to watch. If you'd like to be a part of a production, watch their website for auditions. You can also join Boise Little Theater Student Club. It's for ages 12 to 18. BLT Student Club offers volunteer opportunities at the theater and during community events.

Treasure Valley Children's Theater

Treasure Valley Children's Theater is a nonprofit in Meridian that produces a season of shows for young audiences with a professional, adult acting company. They also offer performing arts training year-round for youth as young as 4 years old. The company's Theater for Young Performers series immerse youth ages 8-18 in the creative process of preparing a high-quality performance for the community while also teaching leadership and life skills rooted in the organization's five core values: Respect, Courage, Commitment, Enthusiasm and Excellence.

Wassmuth Center for Human Rights

Anne probably never heard of Boise, but Boise will not forget her. Her struggle for basic human dignity and the struggles of others are honored at the Wassmuth Center for Human Rights and Boise's Anne Frank Human Rights Memorial. It is the only Anne Frank Memorial in the United States.

Anne Frank

Anne Frank was 13 when she began writing her famous diary. It is full of the everyday concerns of a teenager, family relationships, insecurities, and what she wanted to be when she grew up. But she would not grow up. Anne died at age 15 in a concentration camp a few months after she made the last entry in her diary. Her profound insights that came while she hid from Nazis in an attic shine an important light on the humanity of the victims of the Third Reich.

Museums

Boise Art Museum

BAM, sounds like an explosion, right? It stands for Boise Art Museum. No explosions here, but plenty for kids to do. They have family activity packs that include games and stories for ages 4-12. Get one whenever you go. Check out the ARTexperience Gallery, an interactive space where those 12 and under can investigate how art is made. Bring an adult along. They'll have fun, too. BAM is in Julia Davis Park across from the main library. Or, as we say in Boise, Library!

Black History Museum

The Idaho Black History Museum is housed in the historic St. Paul Baptist Church building in Julia Davis Park. One special exhibit is called From Slave to President. It's a series of nine 4' x 2' panels by Idaho artist Pablo Rodriguez, Jr. He was inspired to create the work by the election of President Barack Obama. In addition to exhibits and community outreach, popular events include the Annual Gospel Workshop and Concert, and Juneteenth: 'National Freedom Day'.

Idaho State Museum

Opening in 2018, the new Idaho State Museum will lead visitors through the history of Idaho. Journey with Lewis and Clark, Sacagawea, York and the other members of the Corps of Discovery. Travel along in time with Native Americans, mountain men, missionaries, gold miners, and loggers. You can see and touch objects that were important to the Idaho story. Try out different kinds of saddles and put your hands on a giant hydraulic mining nozzle. Next door explore the pioneer village of old time buildings, and walk along the Discovery Trail.

Idaho Penitentiary

The Old Idaho Penitentiary opened in 1872, and held some of the West's most notorious criminals. Today, you can experience over 100 years of Idaho's unique prison history with a visit to "Siberia" (solitary confinement), the dark cell blocks, and the gallows. You'll see 30 historic buildings, some of which burned in a prison riot. Relive the Old Pen's past of daring escapes, scandals and executions. Pro tip: Get a selfie behind the bars!

35

City of Trees

Boise is called the City of Trees because there are a lot of them. Also because early French explorers looking for beavers called out "Les bois, Les bois!" when they first saw the cottonwood trees along the river from the bench above. Les bois means the trees or the woods in French. Captain Benjamin Bonneville's men had walked across miles of sagebrush desert and were happy to see the trees because they knew there would be water nearby.

The Anne Frank Tree

The Anne Frank Memorial includes a chestnut grown from the seed of a tree she often talked about in her famous diary. One passage reads, "The two of us looked out at the blue sky, the bare chestnut tree glistening with dew, the seagulls and other birds glinting with silver as they swooped through the air, and we were so moved and entranced that we couldn't speak." Only 11 saplings came to the US from the original tree.

The Gernika Tree

On the Basque Block, the Cyrus Jacobs-Uberuaga Boarding House has a large tree out front that came from the Gernika'ko Arbola or Tree of Gernika. The original oak in the Basque Country has been replanted several times from saved acorns. The resilience of the Tree of Gernika is legendary. In 1937 the city of Gernika was carpet-bombed by Spanish, fascist dictator Francisco Franco, killing about 1,000 citizens and leveling the town. The Tree of Gernika remained intact.

The Boise Gernika tree

was planted in 1988. It is still healthy and has a robust crop of acorns each year.

By the numbers:

The Boise Parks and Recreation Department takes care of more than 45,000 trees in the city parks and on city property along streets. Many thousands more are on private property in Boise. Would you like to volunteer to count them?

Special Sequoia

One of the most beloved trees in Boise is the giant sequoia that stands on the St. Luks property on Jefferson St. It was planted in 1912 as a seedling sent to Boise by John Muir. The 98-foot-tall tree sported Christmas lights for many years. In the mid-80s arborists discovered that the lights had killed the top of the tree. They did some surgery, redirecting a healthy branch to serve as a new top. That's what gives it the odd shape, almost as if a small tree is growing out of a large one.

B.U.G.S.

At Boise Urban Garden School (BUGS), you'll learn about bugs- which ones are friendly to gardens and which ones you want to keep out - but the focus is on growing things. The summer camp gardening programs include Sprouts for ages 5 to 8, Seed to Harvest for ages 9 to 12, and What's Cookin' University for ages 10 to 14. Teens in the Garden is their summer volunteer service. During the school year they host field trips in their outdoor garden classroom and visit classrooms around the valley. BUGS also helps schools set up their own gardens.

Inside Out

Jim Hall Foothills Learning Center

The Boise Foothills are magical. You often don't notice them, then just before sunset the shadows pop and you can no longer ignore the rolling formations. Or, watch the foothills turn into mountains when the first light snowfall dusts the sagebrush above the frost line. The Foothills Learning Center is in the heart of this community, offering environmental education programs to spark interest in natural resources, science, and Idaho's cultural and ecological heritage.

Idaho Botanical Garden

You'd expect the plants and trees at the Idaho Botanical Garden, but you might not expect Sacajawea. That young woman who was so important to the Corps of Discovery is cast in bronze amidst many of the plants discovered and named by Lewis and Clark. Make sure to check out the giant pencil in the Children's Adventure Garden near the big treehouse. Play a tune on the pipe sculpture by slapping the ends of the pipes with flip-flops.

The Discovery Center

It's all about science! The permanent exhibit at the Discovery Center of Idaho features a ton of hands-on experiments about physics. There's always a new reason to go because they bring in new exhibits all the time. We can't say what will be there when you read this, but we can say past travelling exhibits have included the MythBusters, H2Who!, Sue the tyrannosaurus rex, robotics, and DaVinci! Be sure to find out what their current exhibit is. They have special STEM programs for schools, too.

Boise WaterShed

Why visit a water treatment facility? Because it's a blast! We can't get along without water. Find out where water comes from, how we get it into pipes, what happens when it goes down a drain, and how it is renewed before it goes into the river. Plus, there's a lot of fun art. One sculpture lets you control the water coming out of a dam. What would a tree look like if you built it out of faucets and valves and pipes? You'll never have to ask again. Bring your camera so you can get a selfie "falling" into the center of the earth.

Boise WaterShed by the Numbers:

71% of our planet is covered with water

97% of earth's water is salt water

Idahoans use 162 gallons of water per day

It takes 1,000 gallons of water to make a pair of jeans.

It takes 33 gallons of water to produce an apple

It takes 76.6 gallons of water to produce a potato

41

Zoo Boise

Zoo Boise is a place to see animals and a place where you can help save them. Part of your admission fee goes to help support Gorangosa National Park in Mozambique, Africa, where elephants, lions, crocodiles, and other cool critters live in the wild. Visitors to Zoo Boise have raised more than $2 million for Gorangosa.

More Than A Zoo

Part of every admission goes to the Zoo Boise Conservation Fund which supports the protection of wild animals in Idaho and around the world. Why? Many of our favorite wild animals are in serious trouble. If you take the combined wild population of elephants, lions, tigers, rhinos, gorillas, chimpanzees, orangutans, polar bears, giant pandas, hippos, and giraffes, the total is less than the population of the State of Idaho. If you remove elephants from that list, the total is less than the number of people living in the Treasure Valley.

Zoo Teens

Are you wild about animals? Zoo Boise depends on dedicated volunteers to provide a fun, educational, and conservation-driven experience for everyone who comes through the gate. ZooTeens assist animal care staff, aid with education programs, greet guests, and help with special events. Whatever your talents and reasons for volunteering, Zoo Boise has a place for you. No prior animal experience required, but a passion for wildlife and conservation is.

Animal Encounters

Who doesn't like to be fed? At Zoo Boise you can participate in several animal encounters where you can feed lettuce to a giraffe, meal worms to a sloth bear, and treats to goats, sheep, and llamas. Or, in the summer, you can go on a conservation cruise. You'll board a solar-powered boat for a trip around the lagoon where you'll see patos monkeys and endangered white-backed vultures. It costs a little bit to participate in these activities. The money goes to the Zoo Boise Conservation Fund.

Ridge to Rivers

The System

There are more than 190 miles of trails in the foothills above Boise. Some are for hiking, some are for biking, and there are some designated for motorized use. If you have a horse, you can also find trails to ride. If you use a wheelchair, you're welcome on any of the trails, but they have a list of trails that will be more fun on the Ridge to Rivers website. Why do they call it Ridge to Rivers? The foothills are the ridge part. The trails there tie in with bike and walking paths that lead to the Greenbelt, which is along the Boise River.

Hiking Trails

There are many trails that first-timers and families will like. Start off with easy, flat hikes and work your way up to more difficult terrain. Stay on the trails to avoid poison ivy and the occasional snake. A good place to start is to travel north on 8th street until it turns into a gravel road. There are a couple of parking places along the road and the Foothills Learning Center is there.

Mountain Bike Loops

There are all kinds of fun loops for mountain biking in the foothills. Pick an easy one, or challenge yourself. Follow the wild switchbacks and whoop down the hills. Remember, though, you're not the only one up there.

Motorbike, ATV, and E-Bike Trails

There are several trails where you can ride a motorbike or ATV. That's where you can ride your E-bike. Make sure you're on a trail that is designated for motorized use. Ride those trails, but don't go off of them. They're strict about that.

Dog On and Off-Leash Trails

You can take your dog just about anywhere on the trail system. Be sure to take your leash, though. There are places where you can let the pup loose, if your dog isn't aggressive and you maintain control. Several trails require that your dog is on leash. Always take a plastic bag with you. You know why. Don't forget water for the hound.

Trail Etiquette

This isn't about saying please and thank you. Trail etiquette is all about getting along with other users so everyone can have a good time.
- Stay on the trails
- Move to the side when resting
- Don't use trails when they are wet
- Respect other users

Faster trail users approaching from behind will often say "On your left." That means you should stay to your right until they pass. All trail users should yield to horses, so stop and let them go by.

There's more to learn, so pick up a brochure from any of the Ridge to Rivers partners, the City of Boise, Ada County, the Bureau of Land Management Four Rivers Field Office, the Boise National Forest, and the Idaho Department of Fish and Game.

Wheels

The Greenbelt

Boise is all about the Greenbelt. It runs all the way through town, through parks, BSU, and beside neighborhoods. You can walk or bike alongside the river for miles and miles. Most of the path is paved. There are special wildlife areas that are gravel walking paths.

The Distance and Orientation Trail System (DOTS)-- see what they did there?-- is a series of 20-inch white spots painted on the Greenbelt's surface every tenth of a mile. Inside the white spots are black numbers that tell you how far the spot is from zero – the 8th Street pedestrian bridge in Downtown Boise. Walking or biking the Greenbelt is the number one thing on your Boise Bucket List.

Boise Bicycle Project

The Boise Bicycle Project has a BIG idea. The folks there think Boise can be the cycling capital of America. They're doing their part by making affordable bikes available to everyone. They also give a lot of bikes away to kids who can't afford to buy one. How? They get donated bikes that need some work and they fix them up. A kid can draw the bike they want, and the volunteers get started building it. It's like working at the North Pole!

Rhodes Skate Park

What do you do with the concrete space beneath a busy overpass? Boise created a skatepark cool enough to be an X-Games site. Rhodes Skate Park is between 15th and 16th streets under the I-184 connector. You can skateboard, ride your BMX bike, show your scooter tricks, and practice parkour. Parkour (pronounced par-coeur, if you didn't know) is using whatever is handy--steps, benches, walls, rails--as an obstacle course. You can check out what's going on at Rhodes Skate Park anytime on several webcams.

Boise Green Bike

If your family finds itself downtown without bicycles, don't panic! There are racks of bikes available that you can rent to tour around town and on the Greenbelt. First, grab the app at boise.greenbike.com. It will guide you to the bikes and explain how it works.

The Boise Bicycle Project by the numbers:

Volunteers: 3,000
Free bikes for kids: more than 5,000

49

Winging It

Back From the Brink

What's a California condor doing in Boise? Getting some help staying alive. The condors were dying because they were eating a lot of lead from birds and animals that had been shot. There were only 22 California condors left in the world in 1982, so they needed help. The World Center for Birds of Prey knew how to do that. They started raising condors in big cages. The captive breeding program is working. Today there are more than 400 California condors. About half have been freed into the wild. That's still not a lot, so the World Center continues its work to bring these and other birds of prey back from the brink of extinction. Oh, and yes, you can go see them.

California Condors by the numbers:

Wingspan: 9-1/2 feet

Weight: up to 26 pounds

Lifespan: up to 50 years

World Center for Birds of Prey

The World Center for Birds of Prey is just south of Boise. You'll probably see raptors in the wild outside the center. You can also see them inside during live presentations throughout the day - falcons, hawks, and sometimes eagles with their talons clamped around someone's arm. Find out how the Peregrine Fund, which runs the center, works to save species from extinction.

Do you want to know how people hunt with falcons? They do presentations on that, and they have one of the largest collections of literature on birds in the world.

Intermountain Bird Observatory

Birds have the whole sky to fly in. Even so, there are certain routes that many migrating birds follow. The Boise Ridge near Lucky Peak is one of only a few locations in the western U.S. where great numbers of raptors, songbirds, and forest owls concentrate during their fall migration. That makes a great spot for the Intermountain Bird Observatory to band birds. You can learn how they do that and maybe even watch. They'll explain why birds love this spot so much.

Butterflies in Bloom

During the summer, you get to step inside the Zoo Boise butterfly enclosure and walk around with hundreds of Costa Rican butterflies. They're all different colors, shapes, and sizes. New ones frequently arrive from Costa Rican butterfly farmers. Your admission fee helps support programs to raise butterflies and preserve their habitat. Pro tip: Go during the heat of the day and wear bright clothes if you'd like them to land on you.

The Morley Nelson Snake River Birds of Prey National Conservation Area

You still want to see more raptors? About 45 minutes from downtown Boise the deep canyon of the Snake River, with its crags and crevices and thermal updrafts, is home to the greatest concentration of nesting birds of prey in North America. Here habitat is preserved so the birds can live free. Viewing is better at certain times of the year. Ask about it while you're at the World Center for Birds of Prey.

Fins

The MK Nature Center

Okay, so you're practically downtown. You wouldn't expect to see a deer, would you? You can often see a wild deer at the MK Nature Center. That's because they built it to provide habitat for wild critters. They put paths for you through the bushes, brush, and trees, across footbridges over fish ponds, and provided a place to sit down and watch fish through a viewing window. Inside the center you can make animal tracks in the sand, touch fur pelts, handle horns, antlers and skulls. All the plants and animals found here are native to Idaho.

Aquarium of Boise

Most of what swims, slithers, or crawls at the Aquarium of Boise is exotic. That means the animals don't naturally live here. Sharks, for instance. You don't have to worry about sharks in the Boise River. You can see one, though, at the Boise Aquarium. Check out the shark and pufferfish pool, the shark and ray pool, and the Amazon exhibit. The Amazing Angels exhibit is a reef where you can feed and touch tropical fish. There's a tide pool where you can search for sea urchins, sea stars, and Spanish lobsters. The aquarium also has an exotic bird aviary where you can interact with colorful parrots and other feathered friends.

Where to Fish

The Boise River is always a good bet. Sometimes they plant steelhead trout in the river! Riverside pond at the corner of Glenwood Road and Riverside drive has good bank fishing. Veterans Park Pond, and Quinn's Pond are both along the Greenbelt in city parks. Park Center Pond is just off Park Center Boulevard east of the Park Center Bridge.

Getting Legal

If you're under 14 you don't need a fishing license if you live in Idaho. If you don't live here, you can still fish without a license under 14 if you are with someone who has one. You can get a license just about anywhere they sell tackle. The Fish and Game office on Warm Springs has them for sure.

Splash

Beaches

Boise's got 'em. Technically a couple of them are just outside the city. The beach at Eagle Island State Park is sandy and the water is wet. What else do you need? You can rent stand-up paddleboards (SUPs), play on the waterslide, picnic, play disc golf, and ride the zipline course. At Lucky Peak State Park, Sandy Point Beach is right at the foot of Lucky Peak Dam. There's a fountain in the middle of the lake where you can cool off, and you can picnic and disc golf when you're tired of sunbathing. In town, check out the beach at Quinn's Pond. You can swim, paddleboard, kayak, and fish in the lake. The Boise Whitewater Park and the Greenbelt are right there on the edge of the park.

Whitewater

Boise's Whitewater Park is a great place to improve your kayak and SUP skills. Staff can control the adjustable waveshapers to create different conditions on a 20-foot wide primary wave and a 25-foot secondary wave. It's all done with giant air bladders. You can watch it all on a webcam. If you want to take a longer ride down a terrific whitewater river, you'll need to go about an hour out of town to float the Payette River.

Float

Here's something you can't do in just any town. Float the river! During the summer months you can float from Barber Park to Ann Morrison Park. Rent tubes, or rafts, or kayaks at Barber Park, then take a shuttle back to the car when you're done floating about an hour and a half later. You'll want to hone your splashing skills and maybe even bring a Super Soaker. Everyone gets a personal floatation device when you rent your toys.

Pro tip: wear your flotation device. The Boise River runs slow during float season, but it's easy to get pulled into the water by branches or fall out of the boat.

SLIDES

Do you want to slide? How do these names grab you? Corkscrew, Cliffhanger, Thunder Falls, Viper's Vortex, Mammoth Canyon, Pipeline Mines, Avalanche, Rattlesnake Rapids, Racing Ridge, and Double Trouble Drop Slide. They're all waterslides at Roaring Springs Water Park, about 15 minutes from downtown by car off I-84 at the Meridian exit. They have the best surf in Idaho at the White Water Bay Wave Pool. Wahooz Family Fun Zone is right next door.

POOLS

If you need serious cooling, Boise has seven swimming pools, the Boise Natatorium and Hydrotube, the Aquatics Center at the West Family Y, Borah Pool, Fairmont Pool, Ivywild Pool, Lowell Pool, and South Pool.

Grove Plaza

If you just want to cool off, that's what the fountain in Grove Plaza is all about. Splash around, then count the bricks.

Grove Plaza by the Numbers:

- Total Brick Count – 247,500
- Engraved Bricks – 18,334
- It is a 200' diameter circle
- There are 25 jets in the fountain
- The fountain cistern holds 8,000 gallons of water

Up There

Table Rock

You can drive to the top of Table Rock or take a hike! Go to the Old Idaho Penitentiary and park there. The trail is 3.8 miles. Some of it is a little steep, but it is not considered difficult. You'll see wildflowers if you go in the spring. Take your dog along as long as you hang on to that leash. Once you're up there, just look around. You'll see why Boise is called the City of Trees. Also, go look down into the quarry on the east end of Table Rock. Rocks from here went into the Old Penitentiary, the Idaho Capitol, and many other buildings.

The Statehouse & Boise Train Depot

You can take the elevator to the top floor of the capitol building or the bell tower of the Boise Train Depot. Whichever you choose, you'll be looking at the other one. The Capitol and the Boise Depot are at opposite ends of Capitol Boulevard.

Bogus Basin

To get up high above the city, go to Bogus Basin, summer or winter. The base of the ski hill is at 6,150 feet. You'll be able to see into Oregon! Those mountains to the south and west are called the Owyhees.

You Say Hawaii, I Say Owyhee

Owyhee, as in the Owyhee Mountains, may make you think of beaches and palm trees. Owyhee is an old spelling of the word Hawaii. Three fur trappers from Hawaii disappeared in those mountains in 1819. They never got to go home, but because of them their home islands and a place in Idaho share a name with different spellings.

High-Flying Firefighters

During the summer in Boise, you can often hear the roar of C-130s because Boise is home to the National Interagency Fire Center (NIFC). Those planes are probably on their way to drop 3,500 gallons of red retardant on fires in Idaho, Oregon, or Nevada. The men and women at NIFC coordinate wildland firefighting all across the country from their headquarters near the Boise airport. The Wildland Firefighters National Monument is located on the grounds of NIFC, 3833 Development Avenue.

HOT!

Geothermal Heat

Boise has the largest municipal geothermal energy system in the country. It started in 1890 and is one of the oldest hot water heating systems in the world. How hot is it? Too hot to take a bath in, unless you cool it down. It comes out of the ground at 170 degrees. Boise has 20 miles of pipeline circulating 300 million gallons a year. Many downtown buildings, including city hall and the capitol building are heated geothermally. Boise State University is also on the system.

The Natatorium

If you want to experience Boise's hot water up close and personal you can just turn on a faucet in the capitol building. But if you really want to get into it visit the Natatorium. You can swim in the 240,000-gallon pool or zip down the waterslide. The Natatorium is on Warm Springs Avenue. It's not a big secret why the street is named Warm Springs. The houses there were the first to be served by Boise's geothermal well.

Steam Tractors

There are 10 or 11 steam traction engines among the 50 or so tractors at JUMP! Tractors like these ripped up sod in the Midwest from Canada to Mexico. They let farmers plant a lot of crops in the early part of the 20th Century. Can you think of a downside to that? Hint: dust. One of the big guys at JUMP is the 1913 Port Huron. It weighs about 23,000 pounds, is 11 feet tall and 19 feet long. Its rear wheels are almost six feet high. The 100 HP tractor is one of only four left in the world.

Big Mike

Hot water, in the form of steam, ran the railroads years ago. Giant locomotives like Big Mike at the Boise Depot pulled thousands of train cars. There were 14,000 locomotives just like Big Mike built between 1911 and 1944. This locomotive was called a Mikado-type because the first ones were built for export to Japan. Railroad men nicknamed them Mike. Boise's Big Mike was built in 1920. It was a model 282, which meant it has eight big wheels with two more in front and two in back.

Big Mike by the Numbers:

Fuel: soft coal

Boiler pressure: 210 psi

Cylinder diameter & stroke: 26" & 28"

Driving wheel diameter: 63"

Horse power: 3,500

Weight of engine: 463,000 lbs

Length of engine & tender: 81'-9 1/2"

Height to Stack: 15'-10 3/8"

Coal capacity: 17 tons

Water capacity: 10,000 gallons

Weapons of War

Idaho Military History Museum

There's an Idaho connection to just about everything here. Did you know one of the largest Naval Training Stations in the country during World War II was in Idaho? Yes, the NAVY, picked Idaho to train sailors. They used Lake Pend Oreille near Coeur d'Alene to train more than 292,000 recruits. There's still a Navy base there where they test submarine designs. Oh, and how about this: For years, all the sailors getting ready to serve on nuclear submarines trained in Idaho- in the desert! Find out about all this, Idaho's Medal of Honor Winners, and the USS Boise.

The Mikoyan-Gurevich MiG-21 at the Idaho Military History Museum was flown by the Polish Air Force before it was decommissioned. This is the same model flown by the Soviet Union starting in 1959. It is painted now with the markings of MiG-21s flown by Russia. There were 11,496 of these made. They could fly at more than 58,000 feet at a speed of 1,350 mph. Where else can you put your hands on a MiG?

Warhawk Air Museum

Airplanes from World War I, World War II, and the Cold War era are central to the collection at the Warhawk Air Museum in Nampa. See a P-51 Mustang, a Huey helicopter, a Starfighter, and more. There are thousands of artifacts that tell personal stories and help honor veterans. You'll want to plan on spending at least a couple of hours here.

J. Curtis Earl Memorial Exhibit

This is one of largest collections of historic arms and military items in the country. It is housed in one of the buildings at the Old Penitentiary, and doesn't cost extra to see it. Here you can strap on the VR goggles and experience World War I bullets flying overhead while you return fire. Then, take a look at the weapons that were used in that war and other conflicts throughout history. Weapons dating back 3,500 years are on display, along with an 1883 Gatling gun, medieval arms and armor, Revolutionary War firearms and swords, cannons, and more!

CREEPY

BOO

Not scared yet? Maybe a visit to the old Idaho Penitentiary will change that. There's no guarantee of seeing a ghost, but the dark old buildings where men and women lived and died is major spooky. Legend has it that an inmate sentenced to death got loose and climbed into the rafters. They couldn't talk him into coming down. After a while he shouted that "I have a right to choose the way I die!" He then jumped to his death. Seems like a good candidate for a haunting, don't you think?

BOO II

A man named Raymond Snowden was known as Idaho's Jack the Ripper. He had been convicted of murder and sentenced to hang. The hanging did not go well. First, when the trap door dropped down, the rattling caused the gallows observation window to shatter. Meanwhile, the hanging did not break Snowden's neck as is the hoped-for outcome of such events. He struggled at the end of the rope for 15 minutes before finally giving up the ghost.

BUG DAY

Let's say you've caught a bug and don't know what to call it. Sure, you can call it Waldo because you like that name, or you could find out what scientists call it. Okay, maybe they'd call it Waldo, too, but they'll also have a scientific name and a common name for bugs like that. Finding out about bugs is what Bug Day at the Idaho Botanical Gardens is all about. Watch for it every August. You'll be able to catch a bug and take it to an entomologist (insect scientist), who may or may not be called Waldo, and have them tell you all about it. You can even earn a Certificate of Bugology.

Urban Worm

Worms are not something you'd expect to find in a restaurant. Okay, they're not in the restaurant, they're beneath it - in the basement. There are exactly 3.5 kajillion worms living under the floor at Redfeather Lounge and Bittercreek Alehouse. Or, maybe more like 200,000. The restaurant was the first in the U.S. to vermicompost, which means they recycle food scraps in giant worm bins the size of industrial dumpsters. They even print their menus on paper the worms will like so they can recycle those when they get worn out. You've got to see this.

Zoo Boise

Sure, you'll see the fluffy stuff like the red pandas and the tall and cool stuff, like giraffes, but if you want your fill of creepy and/or crawly, Zoo Boise can do it. Check out the Madagascar hissing cockroaches and the tailless whip scorpions. Gila monsters are monsterish, for sure, but not as cringe-worthy as a komodo dragon. Those puppies can get to be ten feet long! Snakes and snakes and snakes, of course. The on-the-edge critters are in the arthropod and reptile exhibits.

Urban Worm uses red wriggler worms to turn things "from spoil to soil." They can tell you how to get started with your own worm farm to take care of kitchen waste. All of their worms are named Steve, except for Big Bertha, Velvet, and Moaning Myrtle. So, when you talk to them, just go with "Steve." That's easier than their scientific name, which is Eisenia fetida.

Park It!

Ann Morrison

Harry Morrison donated Ann Morrison Park in honor of his wife Ann in 1959. The Morrison Knudsen construction company, which also built Hoover and Lucky Peak dams, built the 153-acre park. It has tennis courts, lighted softball diamonds, and fields for soccer, cricket, and football. You can play disc golf, use the outdoor gym, play horseshoes, walk your dog, feed the ducks, access the Greenbelt, and sometimes listen to concerts. This is where you pull your tube or raft out of the river when you've floated from Barber Park upstream.

Julia Davis

Three parks are at the core of the Boise City Parks system, each of them named after women. They are the central gems in Boise's "Ribbon of Jewels" parks along the Greenbelt. Julia Davis Park is the oldest in the system. It was given to the city by her husband Thomas Davis, an early settler, in 1907. At nearly 90 acres, it contains Zoo Boise, Boise Art Museum, Idaho State Museum, Idaho Black History Museum, and Discovery Center of Idaho. The Boise River and the Greenbelt hug along the south side with a footbridge that leads to BSU.

Kathryn Albertson

Kathryn Albertson Park was donated by grocery store pioneer Joe Albertson in honor of his wife. Dedicated in 1989, the park is a 41-acre nature preserve with paved footpaths that tie into the Greenbelt. The pathways wind by a series of ponds and islands where you'll spot ducks, geese, heron, yellow-headed blackbirds, aquatic insects, and dragonflies. Two stone gazebos are used as outdoor classrooms, bird watching platforms, and favorite places for family photos. Golden Eagle Audubon often leads birding tours here.

Boise Parks by the numbers:

90 park sites

25 miles of Greenbelt in the city limits

50 miles of Greenbelt total

200 miles of foothills trails

45,000+ city trees

1600 acres of land

77 playgrounds

86 tennis courts

7 recreation centers

6 outdoor swimming pools

5 dog parks

3 skate parks

2 golf courses

BOGUS BASIN

Bogus Basin is called that because some early prospectors tried to pass off iron pyrite or "fool's gold" from that area as the real thing.

Summer or Winter

Check the temperature. Is it below freezing? If so, you can probably go downhill skiing at Bogus Basin, or snowboard, or cross-country ski. Is the temperature closer to 90? If so, the winter stuff is out. It's summer! You can still go tubing. Take a tube down a slippery synthetic surface. Race side-by-side down two 300-foot lanes at 25 miles per hour. Get a train of tubes going. When you reach the bottom hop on the lift for a ride back to the top.

Bungee Trampoline

Can you fly 20 feet in the air on your trampoline? You can really get up there on the bungee trampoline at Bogus Basin. Do back flips and front flips and twists and turns and don't worry about falling. You're strapped into a secure harness with bungee cords all around. The harder you bounce the higher you go!

Mountain Coaster

The Glade Runner Mountain Coaster twists and turns for 3400 feet at speeds up to 25 miles per hour. You'll think you're going a hundred! You ride in a cart that lets you control your speed as you zip through the trees, sometimes 40 feet in the air. Each cart can carry a driver and a rider. Ride the coaster summer or winter.

Climbing

Are you into climbing? They have a 32-foot structure at Bogus where you can try four different climbing routes. You strap into an auto belay system that takes up the slack as you climb and makes sure you don't fall. When you're ready to come down, it lets you down easy. How fast can you climb? There's a timer so you can race a buddy or race yourself.

Winter

Long-time Boiseans will tell you the snow "doesn't stick." That means that, sure, it snows here, but it usually melts off in a day or two. Then they'll tell you about the winter they had to use sled dogs to get to work. You can play in the snow in Boise, sometimes. Sled off Camel's Back when conditions are right. Mostly, you'll want to go where the snow is in the winter.

BOGUS BASIN

There's so much cool stuff to do in the summer (page 70) that it's easy to forget this is a ski area. You can downhill on your board, your skis, or a tube day or night. You can cross-country ski on groomed trails, and trek across the mountain on snowshoes. Don't know how to ski? They can teach you! Not into walking up mountains? That's what the lifts are for.

Park N' Ski

Park N' Ski, operated by the Idaho Department of Parks and Recreation, has 17 sites across the state where you can—wait for it—park and ski! You can cross-country ski and snowshoe on groomed trails. Four of the areas are just above Idaho City, about an hour out of Boise. They are Banner Ridge, Gold Fork, Whoop-Um-Up, and Beaver Creek Summit. You can even stay overnight in a yurt, but you'll need reservations.

Snowmobiling

Idaho has—no kidding—thousands of miles of groomed snowmobile trails. The closest ones to Boise are near Lowman and around Cascade. Check with a local snowmobile dealer to find out more.

Book It

Library!

About that exclamation point: It's there because Boise libraries are exciting. They have something scheduled for kids every single day. You probably know you can check out books and videos. You might not have known you can check out a Kidpack at the main library. They are for pre-school and elementary kids. Each Kidpack is filled with things from Airplanes to Zoo animals. They include a variety of things on different topics, such as books, DVDs, CDs, puppets, and puzzles. Parents can check them out for two weeks.

Rediscovered

Tons of books. Rows of books. Books by the bushel. How do you like to measure them? Rediscovered Books also has special events for kids and author readings all the time. Join other kids in a book club. They've got one for fourth through sixth grade and one for Junior High students. And here's a tricky thing, almost like platform 9 3/4. Rediscovered is at 180 N 8th Street, and 701 West Idaho Street. Don't panic. It's all the same store.

The Cabin

The Cabin is called that because it is in a log building next the main Boise Library! It is a literary center that supports local writers and brings popular writers to town for talks. Kids like to write, too, so the cabin runs a program called Writers in the Schools. They employ professional local writers—poets, novelists, playwrights, and journalists—to teach semester- or school-year-long writing residencies in schools, juvenile detention centers, and community learning centers.

When summer rolls around, The Cabin sponsors summer writing camps for grades 3-12.

Writers at Harriman

Boise-based Writers at Harriman is a summer writing camp for high school students. Young writers from all over Idaho spend a week at Harriman State Park of Idaho learning from gifted teaching writers. They also learn from moose, trumpeter swans, and that horse they take on a trail ride. It is affordable, desirable, and unforgettable. Oh, and scholarships are available.

Climbing

Boise Rock Gym

Are you new to climbing? The Boise Rock Gym at the Wings Center might be for you. They're dedicated to groups and special events. They have more than 20 top-rope sections, bouldering, rope ladders, and even tire walls.

The Y

The Y has indoor climbing walls at their West Valley and downtown locations. You can participate in a climbing camp, the Little Monkeys Climbing Class, open climb time, or join the Teen Climbing Club, depending on your age.

Asana Climbing Gym

Asana Climbing Gym has climbing options for kids 6-17, including Summer, Winter and Spring break program, as well as after school programs in cooperation with Boise Parks and Recreation. They can also handle your next birthday party as you crawl the wall to being one year older.

Are you ready for the real thing? There are plenty of places to climb real rocks or go bouldering in the Boise area. Ask local climbers about the Black Cliffs, Table Rock, and the canyon at Swan Falls.

Pro Sports

Steelheads

The Idaho Steelheads hockey team has won two Kelly Cup championships, three western conference titles, had twenty players advancing to the NHL and an average of 41 wins per season since joining the East Coast Hockey League. They play in Century Link Arena downtown.

Treasure Valley Roller Derby

The nicknames say it all: Luna Shovegood, Diva Destruction, Avalanche, Sinister Kate, Scarlet Danger. These women are serious skaters and they're a blast to watch. They play at Expo Idaho. They are a DIY skater-run league, always looking for new players. There's a Junior Gems program you might want to find out about.

Quidditch

If you've read Harry Potter, you know about quidditch. There's a Boise State U.S. Quidditch team called the Abraxans, and beginning in 2018 the Major League Quidditch team, the Boise Grays, will begin playing. Sadly, flying is not allowed on either team. Players must ride brooms, but keep them on the ground. Get that golden snitch!

Boise Hawks

The Boise Hawks has been a baseball team in the Northwest League all the way back to 1975, when the Hawks were first called the Boise A's. Twelve years later, Boise A's became the Boise Hawks while joining forces with the Major League Baseball affiliate, the Anaheim Angels. Today, the Boise Hawks are the Short Season Single-A affiliate of the Colorado Rockies and play at Memorial Stadium near the Western Idaho Fairgrounds.

Family Fun

Fast Track Lanes

Driving at 35 mph doesn't seem very fast unless you're a couple of inches off the floor in a screaming kart. Race your friends while your family watches, or race your family. They're set up for parties, too.

Pojo's

Pojo's has been around since 1974 with tons of arcade games, an indoor carousel, and bumper cars. You can snarf down kid food while you play. If you have a birthday, invite your 40 closest friends.

Idaho Ice World

You can ice skate year around at Idaho IceWorld, operated by Boise City Parks and Recreation. They have public skate sessions, figure skating programs, youth and adult hockey leagues, and everything you need to throw a party. They have two NHL regulation size rinks and a pro shop where you can buy figure skating and hockey equipment.

Jump Time

It's chaos here! Kids are bouncing off the walls and rolling around in balls. They're playing dodgeball, slam dunking basketballs, and practicing their tumbles in the foam pit. Trampolines are everywhere. Grab something to eat or play a videogame while you catch your breath.

Eagle Island Zip Lines

Located in Eagle Island State Park, the course has some of Idaho's longest zip lines, including a triple-wide racing zip line. You go from station to station and ride the lines from one platform to another, for about a one mile tour.

North End

From the 1890s to the 1950s Boise's North End Neighborhood was the main area for residential development. That means most of Boise's older homes are here. They range from modest bungalows to three-story mansions. Some of the bigger homes are on Harrison Boulevard, named after President Benjamin Harrison who signed the act making Idaho a state in 1890.

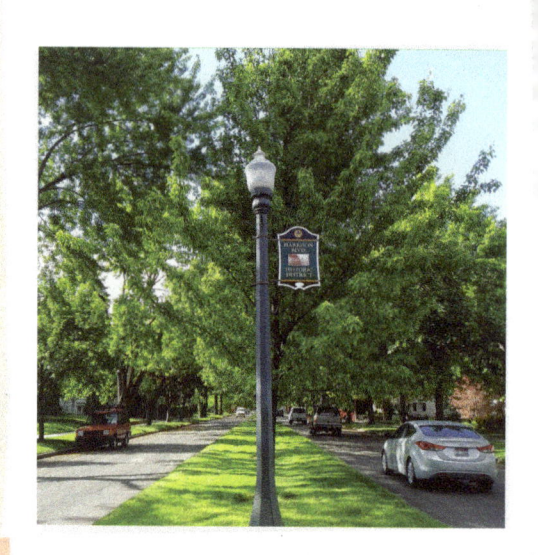

Lay of the Land

The north/south streets are numbered (except for Harrison Boulevard). The east/west streets have names. Boise's nickname is the City of Trees, and you'll see a lot of them when you're in the North End. Many of the trees have been growing here almost since the founding of the city.

Hyde Park

The historic center of the North End is Hyde Park. It's a small business district at about 13th and Eastman. There are several places to eat, including Parilla Grill, 13th Street Pub and Grill, Camel's Crossing, the Hyde Park Pub, Java Hyde Park, Sun Ray Café, Goody's Goodies, North End Pizza, and Casa Mexico. The area has a cycling shop, a salon, a gas station, a barber shop, and specialty markets. You'll see lots of kids and bikes.

Camel's Back Park

One of the most popular places to hang out in the North End is Camel's Back Park. It has grass and trees, which you would expect, but it also has a steep hill that reminded someone of a camel. It isn't very high, but you have to climb it. You'll get a surprising view of the city. You can access the Boise Foothills from Camel's Back, so keep that in mind. The park has tennis courts, a playground, and picnic areas. Bodybuilding.com, which is a Boise company, donated an outdoor gym to the park. Pump up!

G. Willikers

Here's a place where you can't get a lot of things you probably like, such as video games, smartphones, and RC cars. But, wow, they have a ton of things you need to see. G. Willikers is a toy store that specializes in classic toys that require you to have an imagination. Got one? Perfect. G. Willikers is in Hyde Park.

Goody's Goodies

You probably don't like ice cream, or chocolate, or candy, but we'll tell you about a place in the North End where you can get all those things, just in case. Goody's Goodies is in Hyde Park. They have an old-fashioned Soda Fountain where you sit on a stool in front of a counter. They make their ice cream right in the store. It's the same for the chocolate, which has no artificial flavors or ingredients.

Bown's Crossing

To the East

In southeast Boise there's a little business district called Bown Crossing that is fun and walkable (once you drive there)! It's off E Park Center Boulevard at Bown Way. Kids will like Flatbread Pizza, where you can make your own; Cravin's Candy Emporium, where they have a million kinds of candy; and Lucky Bums, where they sell outdoor gear for kids. Boise's newest library is right in the neighborhood.

Bown House

It's a house, it's a school, it's history! The Bown House, with 20-inch sandstone walls quarried from the Table Rock, was built as a home for a ranching family in 1879. Mrs. Bown was a teacher. When the Pioneer School where she taught burned down, she moved classes to her home. The Bowns came to Idaho on the Oregon Trail, which ran right by where the house now stands. It's now a part of the Riverside Elementary School Campus. Use a smartphone to find out about tours.

Day & Night in the Desert

Bruneau Dunes

Bruneau Dunes State Park is a little over an hour from Boise. The biggest dune in the park is 470 feet from the lake at the bottom to the sandy crest. That's the tallest single-structured sand dune in North America. Climb the dunes, fish, hike, slide down the sand on a rental sand board.

Bruneau Canyon

While you're at Bruneau Dunes, you have to drive another 20 minutes to the Bruneau Canyon Overlook. No climbing needed. Just step out of the car and walk up to the edge. Grab the railing. Now, look down, 800 feet to the river below. The cliffs on the far side of the river are 1300 feet away.

In the Dark

Idaho's largest observatory is at Bruneau Dunes State Park. Check the schedule on the web for observatory presentations. Hint: They're usually at night, so you might want to think about renting a cabin or bringing an RV.

Glowing Stingers

The desert comes alive at night. That's when the nocturnal animals come out to eat. You could see coyotes, raccoons, and porcupines. Bring a portable black light and you will see scorpions. They glow in the dark when you shine it on them. They can sting, but they really aren't dangerous.

Camping

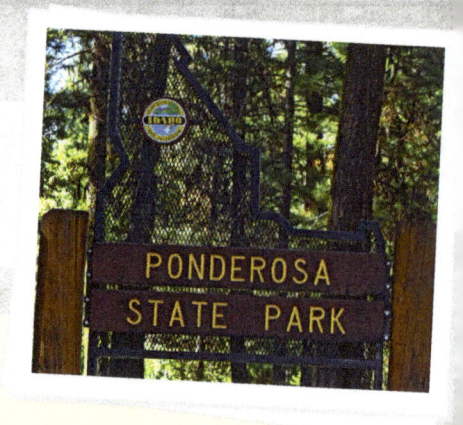

State Parks

There are four state parks where you can camp within a couple of hours of Boise. Ponderosa State Park, in McCall, is on beautiful Payette Lake. They have cabins as well as camping sites. The hiking and biking trails take you up to a steep cliff with views of the lake and wilderness area mountains. Lake Cascade State Park has many campgrounds scattered around the lake. It's all about the boats, here. If your family has one, strap on the water skis.

Bruneau Dunes is about an hour away (see page 88). Three Island Crossing State Park, just outside of Glenns Ferry, has Oregon Trail History. See where the wagons crossed the Snake River at one of the most treacherous points in their journey.

National Parks

The US Forest Service has more rugged campgrounds within an hour or two of Boise. Pick up a copy of the Idaho RV Campground Directory for a complete listing of all the campgrounds in the state. It's free and available at most visitor centers.

Cemeteries

Pioneer Cemetery

Here you can visit the graves of many Boise mayors and some important Idaho governors. One mayor, Cyrus Jacobs, built the house on the Basque Block that is now a museum (Page 13). Learn about Jesus Urquides, who used 35 mules to pack 10,000 pounds of copper wire 70 miles to a mine with the rolls strung together mule to mule without a single break in the wire.

Walking Tours

The Boise City Parks website has information on walking tours for two city cemeteries. Why do you care? Because learning about famous and infamous people can be fun!

Morris Hill Cemetery

Visit the grave of Charles Ostner who carved the horse on page 11. Harry Orchard, Idaho's most famous assassin is there. Joe Albertson and J.R. Simplot, men who built business empires are at Morris Hill Cemetery, along with governors, senators, murderers, and a former director of counterintelligence for the CIA. Don't miss Peg Leg Annie's grave.

Ghost Towns

Silver City

Silver City is about two hours from Boise. Expect gravel roads that may be bumpy. You're really going back in time here. There are about 75 buildings from the 1860s to the early 1900s. This old mining town still has a few permanent residents. Someone has to run Pat's What Not Shop. You'll see cemeteries and headstones because, ghosts, right?

Idaho City

Idaho City is easy to get to from Boise. It's about an hour away on a paved road that takes you past Lucky Peak. During the Idaho gold rush, Idaho City was the biggest city in the Northwest. That didn't last long, because the gold eventually played out. You can walk the boardwalks, go inside historic structures, and have an ice cream and sarsaparilla in the local saloon.

On the Edge
Beyond Boise

WINGS

The Morley Nelson Snake River Birds of Prey National Conservation Area is about an hour out of Boise. It was established by Congress in 1993. North America's highest concentration of nesting raptors can be found in this unique desert environment where the updrafts along the Snake River Canyon provide good gliding for the birds. More than 700 pairs nest each spring. That includes 150-200 pairs of prairie falcons, the highest density in the world. Take binoculars and water with you.

Cleo's Ferry Museum & Trail

Weird. Sure, there are some old buildings associated with the historic ferry that operated near Melba, Idaho, a little over an hour from downtown Boise. It's what's on the outside that will stick in your brain. The trail has sculptures, bird houses, benches, yard art, clever signs, and STUFF. We're not talking about just a few of anything. Hundreds. Thousands. You'll want to spend all day there walking around just shaking your head.

Celebration Park

Celebration Park, about an hour from Boise, is on the edge of the Morley Nelson Snake River Birds of Prey National Conservation area, so you're likely to see raptors. It is Idaho's only archaeological park. Walk through huge basalt melon gravel—from melon sized to Miata sized—deposited by the Bonneville Flood some 12,000 years ago. See petroglyphs, and throw a dart with an atlatl, the way the first peopleNative Americans bridge and learn about mining and railroad history. Camping is available.

Map Rock

This is Idaho's most famous petroglyph rock. It has many symbols and pictures chipped into its surface. There is much debate about what those symbols mean, but Shoshone-Bannock people say it is a map of the Snake River and hunting areas across what is now southern Idaho. From Nampa, travel south on Highway 45. Turn right on Map Rock Road. Travel 7.3 miles to Map Rock, located on the right side of the road.

ICONS

Idanha

Go to 928 W. Main and you might think you've stepped through a magic door to Europe. The castle-like structure opened as the Idanha hotel on Jan. 1, 1901. Today it holds apartments on the upper floors and businesses below. It was named after another fancy hotel in Soda Springs, Idaho. That hotel took the brand name of carbonated water bottled in Soda Springs. During its years as a hotel it hosted many famous guests. Most of them probably rode in Idaho's oldest elevator.

The Crack

We'll probably get in trouble for calling it that, but everyone does. The Crack is a dramatic piece of art that is actually named The River Sculpture, by artist Alison Sky. You can't miss it if you're at the intersection of Front Street and South Capitol Boulevard. It is on the southern corner of the Grove Hotel, lit from within by neon lights. It used to send clouds of steam into the air, but that became too difficult to maintain. Like all art, some people love it and some people hate it. What do you think? Does it remind you of a river?

Boise Train Depot

In 1925 everyone came out for the dedication of the Boise Train Depot. It replaced an older depot downtown. The Spanish-style, stucco structure with its red tile roof is the "you can't miss it" building on the hill overlooking Capitol Boulevard. When you visit, don't miss Platt Gardens in front of the depot and the mosaic in the roundabout. You can't take the stairs, but they will ride you to the top of the tower in an elevator.

O'Farrell House

John A. O'Farrell built a one-room cabin out of cottonwood trees in 1863. The logs weren't very straight, so he flattened them out with a broad axe. He stuffed branches and clay between the logs to keep the wind out. It served his family for about 8 years. In 1912 the cabin was moved across Fort Street from its original location. The first home built in Boise has been at 450 W Fort St ever since.

Betty the Washerwoman

Who knows why people fall in love with something? Betty the Washerwoman has been scrubbing clothes atop a sign on Vista Avenue since about 1950. The sign made sense when Betty first went up - she was advertising a laundromat. Over the years different kinds of businesses have come and gone, changing what the sign advertised, but Betty keeps scrubbing away. She gets new clothes occasionally. People rally to her defense whenever someone suggests retiring Betty. She's even been the star of her own pin-up calendar!

Rudy the Rooster

Betty the Washerwoman has a friend. He's called Rudy the Rooster. He perched atop a sign at Jim's Coffee Shop in Boise's North End starting sometime in the 1960s. When Jim's closed and Rudy disappeared, some Boiseans panicked. To everyone's great relief Rudy showed up one day on top of the sign for the Capri Restaurant at 2520 W. Fairview. Whew!

The Blue Turf

Until 1986 all football fields in the U.S. were green. Some were grass and some were plastic, but all were green, until Boise State University installed blue artificial turf. It was the first field in football history that was any color but green. Some fans started calling it "Smurf Turf." Boiseans love their blue field. College rules allow colors other than green, but the National Football League does not. BSU's school colors are blue and orange. They are called the Broncos, just like that NFL team in Denver. But BSU had the name first.

Buster Bronco

Buster is the official mascot of Boise State University. He's a horse. Well, he's a person in a horse suit who wears a blue jersey with the number 0 on it for football games and an orange jersey with the number 54 for basketball games. He's kind of an old horse. Buster has been around since 1932.

Souvenirs

Taters

If you're visiting Boise, you'll want to take something home with you. Maybe a t-shirt, or something that looks like a potato. Taters near the Grove Plaza has Idaho stuff from postcards to custom gift boxes.

Boise Wearables

If you're all about clever tee's and caps, check Wear Boise at 828 W. Idaho and Banana Ink at 214 N. 9th.

Ward Hooper's Urban Garage

Hooper has art all over Boise. He came up with the geothermal logo you see on buildings downtown and did the art design for the Basque Block. Posters, postcards and a lot of weird old stuff can be found here at 745 W Idaho.

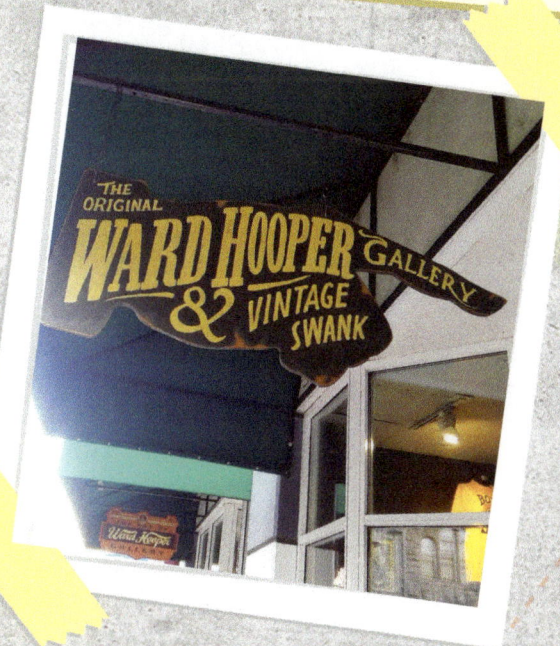

Idaho Made

If you like your stuff handmade, then Idaho Made in Old Boise will work for you. It's a local artists' cooperative!

Walking Around

Walkabout

If you're downtown, here are things within walking distance:

State Capitol
Guru Donuts
Art
The Anne Frank Memorial
The Idaho State Museum
The Idaho Black History Museum
Boise Art Museum
Rediscovered Books
Julia Davis Park
The Greenbelt
JUMP
The Library!
Rhodes Skatepark
Ward Hoopers Urban Garage
Taters

Power Walking

If you don't mind venturing a little further from downtown, you can walk (or drive) to:

The Discovery Center
MK Nature Center
The Boise Depot

Here are a few things that are near each other, You might want to do them on the same trip.

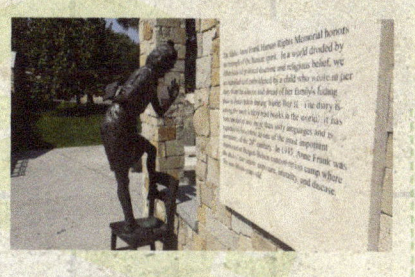

Idaho Black History Museum, Boise Art Museum, Idaho State Museum, Anne Frank Memorial, the Discovery Center.

Idaho Botanical Garden and the Old Pen.

G. Wilikers, Goody's Goodies, Camel's Back Park

Celebration Park and Map Rock.

The Bown House, Cravin's Candy Emporium

Eagle Island State Park and the Eagle Island Fish Hatchery.

The Boise Whitewater Park and Quinn's Pond.

105

Time Out!

One Hour

- Visit Freak Alley Gallery
- Shop at Saturday Market
- Grab a donut at Guru Donuts
- Check out the latest exhibit at Boise Art Museum
- Buy this book (and others) at Rediscovered Books
- Stop and see Ward Hooper's Urban Garage
- Walk through the MK Nature Center
- See Big Mike and the Boise Depot
- Visit the Idaho Black History Museum
- See the Anne Frank Memorial
- Do some cool moves at Rhodes Skate Park

Two Hours

- Tour the capitol building
- Take a tractor tour at JUMP
- Visit the Idaho State Museum
- Do a quick trip to Zoo Boise
- Climb Camel's Back and play in the park
- Discover the Discovery Center of Idaho
- Visit the World Center for Birds of Prey
- Float the Boise River
- Lock yourself up at the Old Pen
- Dress warm for Winter Garden Aglow

Four Hours or More

- Swim at Sandy Point Beach in Lucky Peak State Park
- Ride the zip lines at Eagle Island State Park
- Do the Zoo right
- Visit the Old Pen and the Idaho Botanical Garden
- Explore the trails from the Jim Hall Foothills Nature Center
- Bike the Greenbelt two hours out and (huff, puff) two hours back
- Drive to Idaho City for an ice cream cone and clomp around on the boardwalk

Overnight

Camp at Bruneau Dunes State Park. Try to do it when they're having an astronomy event. Don't forget the s'mores.

Over a Weekend

Camp at Ponderosa State Park in McCall. Take your mountain bike or hiking shoes. Pack your fishing pole. If you have a boat of any kind, drag it along.

Boise Bucket List

> Bucket lists are personal. They're all about what you'd like to do. Here are some things you could do in and around Boise, depending on how much time you have to spend. Mark your top ten.

Some Ideas:

Ride the Greenbelt from end to end.

Experience the Boise outdoor learning centers: MK Nature, Boise Water Shed, Jim Hall Foothills Learning Center, Idaho Botanical Garden.

Ride the Glade Runner Mountain Coaster at Bogus.

Waterski at Lucky Peak.

Skateboard at Rhodes Skate Park.

Experience the Boise indoor learning centers: the Discovery Center, Old Pen, Idaho Historical Museum, Eagle Fish Hatchery

Learn about raptors at the World Center for Birds of Prey, then see where they live at the Snake River Birds of Prey National Conservation Area.

See a movie at the Egyptian.

Mountain bike the Crestline Trail to Lower Hulls gulch.

Swim at Sandy Point, Eagle Island, and the Natatorium.

Float the Boise River.

Go to Art in the Park

Snowshoe Bogus Basin.

X-Country ski Whoop-Um-Up

Climb Camel's Back and take a selfie with Boise in the background.

Ride an SUP at Quinn's Pond

Kayak the waves at the whitewater park.

Tube the hill at Eagle Island in the winter.

Sandboard the big dune at Bruneau Dunes.

Write in some things you want to do.

INDEX

A

Abraham Lincoln   6
Anne Frank Memorial   33, 36
Ann Morrison Park   19, 57, 70
Aquarium of Boise   54
Art in the Park   19
Asana Climbing Gym   79

B

B'ARC Peanut Butter Bones   25
Ballet Idaho   31
Barber Park   57
Basques   12 - 13, 24, 37
Betty the Washerwoman   100
Big Mike   65
Bittercreek / Redfeather   69
Bogus Basin   61, 72-74
Boise Art Museum   34, 70
Boise Bicycle Project   48-49
Boise Contemporary Theater   28
Boise Fry Company   27
Boise Grays   81
Boise Green Bike   49
Boise Greenbelt   44, 48, 56, 70-71
Boise Hawks   81
Boise Little Theater   32
Boise Music Week   31
Boise Philharmonic Youth Orchestra   30
Boise Public Library   18, 76-77
Boise River   44, 54, 57, 70
Boise Rock Gym   78
Boise State University   17, 62, 70, 81, 101
Boise Train Depot   60, 99
Boise Urban Garden Schools (BUGS)   39
Boise Watershed   41
Boise Whitewater Park   56-57
Bown's Crossing   87
Bown House   87
Bruneau Canyon   88
Bruneau Dunes State Park   88-89, 90
Buster Bronco   101

C

Cabin, The   76
California Condor   50
Camel's Back Park 74, 85
Celebration Park   97
Cleo's Ferry Museum &
Trail   96
Comic Arts Festival
18

D

Discovery Center of Idaho
40, 70

E

Eagle Island State park
56, 83
Egyptian Theater   28, 31
Engineering and Science
Festival   17

F

Fast Track Lanes   82
Festival of Trees   21
Fishing   55
Flying Pie Pizza   26
Freak Alley 7
Frisbee Fest 19

G

G. Willikers 86
George Washington 11

Geothermal Heat   62
Gernika Tree   37
Glade Runner Mountain
Coaster   73
Goody's Goodies   86
Grove Plaza 59
Guru Donuts   23

H

Harrison Boulevard
20, 84
Hyde Park   85-86

I

Idaho Black History Museum   34, 70

Idaho Botanical Garden
21, 40, 68
Idaho Capitol Building /
Statehouse 8 - 11, 60
Idaho Centennial   5
Idaho City   75, 95
Idaho County Emblems
5
Idaho Humane Society
19, 25
Idaho Ice World   83
Idaho Made 103
Idaho Military History
Museum   66
Idaho Potato Drop 21
Idaho Shakespeare Festival   29
Idaho Spud Bars   23

111

Idaho State Museum 35, 70
Idaho State Seal 10
Idaho Steelheads 80
Idanha 98
Intermountain Bird Observatory 52

J

J. Curtis Earl Memorial Exhibit 67
Jaialdi 13
Jim Hall Foothills Learning Center 39, 45
Julia Davis Park 6, 19, 34, 70
JUMP (Jask's urban Meeting Place) 14-15, 30, 64
Jump Time 83

K

Kabob House 24
Kathryn Albertson Park 71
Kibrom's Restaurant 26

L

Leku Ona 24
Linder Farms 20
Lucky Peak State Park 52, 56

M

Map Rock 97
MK Nature Center 54
Morley Nelson Snake River Birds of Prey National Conservation Area 53, 96-97

Morris Hill Cemetery 93

N

Natatorium and Hydrotube 58, 63
National Interagency Fire Center 61
National Parks 91
North End 84

O

O'Farrell House 99
Old Idaho Penitentiary 35, 60, 67-68
Old Ninety-Seven 8
Opera Idaho 31
Owyhee Mountains 61

P

Park N' Ski 75
Pioneer Cemetery 92
Pojo's 82

Q

Quinn's Pond 55-56

R

Rediscovered Books 76
Rhodes Skate Park 49
Ridge to Rivers 44-47
River Sculpture 98

Roaring Springs Water Park 58
Rock Climbing 73, 78-79
Rudy the Rooster 100

S

Sandy Point Beach 56
Scentsy Commons Christmas Lights 20
See Spot Walk 19
Silver City 94
Smurf Turf 101
Snowmobiling 75
Spirit of Boise Balloon classic 16
Spring Run 4
St. Lukes Sequoia 38
State Parks 90
Steam Tractors 64
STIL, The 22
Story Story Night 30
Swimming Pools 58

T

Table Rock 60
Tango's 25
Tasty Tales Story Time 23
Taters 102
Traffic Boxes 5
Treasure Valley Children's Theater 32
Treasure Valley Roller Derby 80
Treefort 18
Twilight Criterium 17

U

Urban Worm 69

V

Velma V. Morrison Center for the Performing Arts 31

W

Ward Hooper 103
Warhawk Air Museum 67
Wassmuth Center for Human Rights 33
Wear Boise 102
Western Idaho Fair 17
Winged Victory 10
Winter Garden Aglow 21
World Center for Birds of Prey 50-51
Writers at Harriman 77

Y

YMCA 79

Z

Zoo Boise 42-43, 53, 69-70

PHOTO CREDITS

B
Bogle, Andrea
Bogus Basin
Boise City Department of Arts & History
Boise Hawks
Boise Music Week
Boise Philharmonic
Boise Pro Photo
Boise State University
Boise Urban Garden School
Botkin, Lindsey
Briscoe, Sherry
Budge, Paul
Bureau of Land Management

C
Canyon County Parks and Recreation
Clifford, Simon
Creative Expressions Photography

D
Darnell, Mike
Delaney, Bruce
Dodge, Jen
Downtown Boise Association
Dupree, Summer

F
Flying Pie
Fujii, Dave

G
Garcia, Morgan
Grissom, Andrew
Guru Donuts

H
Haley, Robert
Herbold, Canon
Hilinski, Paula

I
Idaho Candy Co.
Idaho Department of Parks and Recreation
Idaho Fish and Game
Idaho Photographic Arts
Idaho Shakespeare Festival
Irving, AJ
iStock

J
Johnson, David
Johnson, Kaneecia
Laura, Johnston
JUMP
Just, Rick

K
Kimberlee Miller Photography
Kitsinger, Otto
Knopp, Kelly

L
Lightning, Maddox

M
Macey Snelson Photography
McCoy, Emma
McCullough, Mike
Molina, Suki
Murphy, Megan

O
Odermott, Maci
Opera Idaho

P
Parks-Huitron, Heather
Parish, C

R
Rediscovered Books
Reese, Carla
Rigby, Jeremy
Roaring Springs
Rogerson, Austin
Ronayne, Diane

S
Scentsy
Shane, Jim
Shutterhug
Shutterstock
Spurling, Paul
Stinson, Mark
Synchrnyze Photography
Szathmary, Paige

T
The Cabin
Treasure Valley YMCA

U
Urban Ascent

B
Vadenbos, Scarlet
Van Doren, Jane Alice
Vaughan, Maxwell

W
Wassmuth Center for Human Rights

Y
Young, Travis

Z
Zip Boise
Zoo Boise

About the Author

Rick Just is the author of several YA novels, including Ghost Writer, and writes quirky stories about Idaho history on his Facebook page Speaking of Idaho.

About the Designer

I am primarily an illustrator who has built a successful career as a graphic designer. My work has been published locally and internationally; everything from beer labels and snowboards to children's books, illustrations, and apps. Armed with a keen imagination and creative skill, I developed my own style through nontraditional ways and means, guided by trial and error. Primarily working in pen and ink and digital graphic design, I also have a lot of fun experimenting with wood, and other medias. My work is often strange and unexpected, inspired by the narrative of everyday life happenings and personal experiences.

I owe my successes to the talented individuals that I continue to surround myself with. Im always looking forward to the next challenging project to conquer.

knoppart.com

CPSIA information can be obtained
at www.ICGtesting.com
Printed in the USA
LVHW05s0842060618
579721LV00002B/2/P

9 780998 890944